MOSAIC

E.E. KELLY

For you.

Do good things.

Come close, let me tell you

about a feeling I have always had
          a vibration in the core of me

I don't know how else to explain it
          other than that

it is something huge on the horizon
          stampeding towards my life

I don't know when it will get here
          or if it even will

But I think maybe the thrill
          is in the anticipation anyway

MOSAIC

ONE WHOLE CONNECTED THING

You will start to look at your life in parts
the before and the after

This is not right
It is wrong to think that one thing
is significant enough to split your life in two
or that the palm of that hardship
strikes down once
and then pulls away a clean handful

Hardship doesn't take
It leaves

The impact of it
will never be concentrated to one spot
It might turn a duller color
but it will bleed across your entire life

And that is because
a life cannot be broken in two
Your life is just one whole connected thing
that keeps on going
and going

A Wish I Inhale Deep and Then Let Go of

Light floats
across the room
like a whisper
Your breath
traces every edge
of me
Time tumbles
into itself and
pauses
Reality peels
apart
at its seam
This love
finally
finds its way out
into the open

IS THAT TOO MUCH TO ASK?

What do you want from me?
Life whispered
Everything, I replied

DESCENSION

It was only upon peeking back
that I realized how deep in I was back then

Back in the lowest droop of underbelly
in my mediocre life
in the half dead center of suburbia

in the black triangle of woods
behind their house
scattered with sloths and snakes
dense with the sweat of unpleasant memories
lit only by a blubbering campfire, by the glowing ends
of cigarettes

There were graves everywhere
It was hard not to fall into one

So when I did, I did not blame myself

Turns out it was quite easy
laying barebacked, watching it all pass by
cool earth against flesh

When they finally got the shovels
it piled in slowly
so much so that I did not notice at first
and when I did, it was like:

heavy quilt, soothing touch I never felt before,
being needed, becoming an angel,
saving someone

And before I knew any better,
I was buried

THE SKY IS WAITING

Look at the sky
how it hangs there
patiently in the background
Look at how the sky waits for you
Even when the sun and the moon leave
the sky is waiting
You must be patient with yourself
the way the sky is patient
You will take time
to be ready but
when you are
the bright warm sky will be waiting

THEY CALL IT ANXIETY

My earliest memory
is fear—

the soft fuzzy kind
the background noise
the dull diaphragm ache
the constant scratch

Although nothing about my life
was scary
or bad or particularly wrong
it was everywhere

fear. fear. fear.

dark paint strewn across my walls
blood splattered on the soles of my feet
where no one could see
sharp fingernails atop my shoulders
a vice grip around my breath

How do you learn to be a person
when you are scared of people?

How do you find your voice
when you are afraid to speak?

How do you come to grow
when you are scared of
simply living?

NECESSARY RELEASE

I will let go of this
softly and all at once

Love does not always
need to be held
to be felt

IN MY VEINS

Yes it is there
as present as the constant drumming of heart's muscle
the gentle push of full vein beneath skin
a ringing in my ear
the relentless back and forth of breath in, breath out

It's a radiating energy, a gentle reassurance
a growing momentum, a silky sweet promise

a likelihood I can't let go of
a treasure locked tight against my diaphragm

an awakening presence
pulsing
humming
pounding

shouting

reminding:
There is more
There is much better to come

When I Look at You

Let me start with the ending—
I finally realized I'm never getting you back

The better part of a decade and you've been
nothing but water between my fingers

My white-knuckled fists, tight and empty, now
My hope, macerated. And you, mostly
                                  drained out

They say the hardest losses are the sudden ones
But what about when it all pours empty
right. before. your. eyes?

What about the guilt in looking at a face and
forgetting all the good behind it?

What if it was so slow it still takes a few blinks,
and then you remember—*oh right, there was life
here once*?

There was life here. I'd almost forgotten
I'd almost let it all drown

They tell me I can choose what I hold onto
They tell me it doesn't have to cut this deep
They say I can stop clenching this grudge like
an anchor. But nobody ever tells me *how*

It's no use anyway. I already wear my scars.

I sit in the third row at a wedding and tally up
all the things I'll never have
                    in this flash flood life

I walk along the tallest bridge and toss in my very last
wish

You talk to me of your troubles and all I can see is you
wiping away the tears, cleaning up the mess, patting it
all dry

And this is just what I have to live with
This is just how it's going to be
I will never stop seeing what could have been
                    when I look at you

How I've Loved You

I dive into the honey pause
                at the end of your words

mouth closed and sore from this locked
and loaded tongue

Curl myself into the dip in your laugh
chest swelling with
             the thought that I put it there

I choke back confessions
        swallow high-pitched screams

count the letters at the bottom
of my rib cage and

        shudder at their potential impact

Keep quiet, keep closed,
                keep writing

Don't you see?

I have loved you in all the words
            I've never said out loud

YOU HOLD THE ANSWERS

Only your own hands
can piece you back together

FAIRY

You fist fight the bad things with soft hands
When your world is tipping
you tilt your mind on its axis right with it

All of your cries come laced with laughter
You turn hate mail into origami
Where it is dark you put windows

Your soul drips out a little bit into everything you do

And when you hug me
it is like
Fireside in snowstorm
Warm blanket in December
Umbrella on stormy coast
I will be okay

WITH THE BROKEN

They write sweet glitter of me but I am not
a fairytale

There are a million dark strikes hidden beneath
these golden pages

I have learned to keep it all concealed
But I still cannot un-hear the twist and lift at the
ends of their words

My ears bleed until I can only use my eyes
So I watch the leaves let go in autumn
and I wish I could fall to pieces once a year too

It is exhausting being held together by thin lace
and butterfly wings
to paint blush over a black that keeps growing

But the shattering is not dainty and gentle
enough
The real is too open and daunting

They won't stop covering me with soft and
pretty so I will look better

But they cannot wash this question off my skin:
Why are you so afraid of the breaking and
falling
but so obsessed with the broken?

OFFERING OF DAWN

The morning faded navy to champagne sheen
sun's bleeding watercolor
The skies parted like enemies
And the world shouted:
"I am all yours"

SAY GOODBYE TO WHAT YOU KNEW

I've grown weak from the strain of
turning back while running
There were still glimpses of smiles and enough,
of calm streaming through windows,
the sense of belonging even when coming undone
But you took a hand to all of it, eventually

Turns out there are loopholes everywhere
The past can be altered
Nothing is safe
Not even the soft bed where you'd
whisper me to sleep, stroke my hair
(the first and last place I have ever felt loved)

I will see home as a picture, no longer a place
There will be no happy without a sting to it
Even laughter now, in its descent,
holds gravel in it
We can't take back the pain after it
leaves our tongues

FRESH START

Spring will unveil itself gently
and yet it will be loud
the way that change
likes to hang itself next to
your ears and howl
the way a fresh start echoes
open and electric and free
and thick with
possibilities

SUNDAY MORNING

I think you might be rays of sun
floating across the room
Sunday morning

A warm handful of sand
that falls from my palm
grain by grain

A wave that rushes away
just as soon as it covers me

I think you might be something
I will grab at over and over
but never hold on to
for longer than a moment

I think you might be everywhere
and nowhere to be found

Like sunshine
Like air

Over every inch of me
but never in my grasp

Always there
                    hovering

just beyond my reach

RINSE

Stop pouring
all of yourself
out for them

You cannot
rinse away
their hurting

only your own

THEY DAZZLE

Some moments have clean edges
that lay flat against each other without overlap
pretty and neat like a well-constructed home
or a puzzle
Others come to harsh points
they end in corners
like ribbons of flame
like the white-tipped mountain peaks you always
admire
These moments don't end in smooth curves they end in
needles
that insert themselves into the flesh of everything
an injection quick and permanent
a changing
They are ridges on diamonds
reflecting light against every wall
shaking the memory so it dances harsh and infinite
so it cannot be ignored
These moments
they dazzle
they echo
they extend
they command to be remembered
and they make sure you are never the same again

Whose Name is it?

What is it you love most in life?
Picture it

Now, picture it
gone

Bite down at the tongue that
forgets to unfurl its gratitude

Open your mouth, now. What
whisper comes out?

Whose name is it and how many
times does it
bleed?

NARCISSISM BURNS

Maybe the harshest harms
are the subtle ones
The ones you don't intend
but nonetheless inflict on me
while you are busy
regarding only yourself
Maybe what has hurt me most
is the fact that
you have always put
you before me

HELLO; GOODBYE

I am trapped between two palms
that will not move outward
cannot move inward
A moment turns to a moment
turns to an ocean
I cannot put out my hands
so I put out breath
thrust the light from these lungs
step back into darkness
I am made of brick and stone
and morals locked tight
You, of easy sunlight I will never touch
but still feel a million miles away
An entire universe wells up in me
and implodes
Another one dies in my backyard
I cut down my tightrope
cast up hasty walls
burn the ladder
Peel open my face and turn these
eyeballs backwards
paint the irises thick black
Swallow the bitter truth at the
pit of my throat:
I can never look at you through
the same eyes again

To Be Held

Hope is a fragile,
      sturdy thing

A RECOLLECTION OF RECENT MONTHS

In March the wind grew taut and I
watched this thing
    touch down like a tornado

Not long before, in February
I had shouted haphazardly into the
    rippling breeze

        challenged the universe
with loud, fantastic thoughts, like

—Oh, how your hands
        would feel around me

(so much so that they manifested)

    and now

in April, a new color comes finally and
        suddenly and I know
            it to be true that

there is no green like the green
    after winter lifts

        no thrill like that of possibility
        in the distance

    untouchable and

        building

ARRINGTON, TENNESSEE

I wouldn't want to be with anyone else
in this hot heat, air thicker than
these ties between us
There is bright haze and cerulean and the
hope of never letting go
I'm not quite sure I can explain
that I think we are at once wide, expansive
limitless
and unfathomably small
If you want to know what I mean just
look up at this amaranthine sky
Today I swear that blue crept down around us
poured a new world before these eyes
I stay here longer than you think
weave poems around the edges, lock us in tighter
And we come up with words that mean forever
though we know that nothing ever lasts

SELF-DESTRUCTION

Shovel
Padlock
Lead curtains
No, bars
No, only walls
Thick cinder blocks
Six-feet-under-pitch-black
Farthest room
Smallest room
Only me
Soft blanket
Hard realization
Trapped
Only me
Ice on spine chills
Isolated
Hard shell
Barely breathing
Only me
Hands over head
Trapped tight
Only me
Keeper of the shovel:
Only me

Dream to Dust

This morning unfurls a fresh green where
only a breath ago laid white
April pries itself out from its tomb
This newness rests brazenly on my shoulder
as I watch the light pour into the space
where you once stood
The air tastes of hope turned to flesh,
ice turned to Earth, dream turned to dust
All I've ever known of change is that
it is slow and sudden

FROM THE MIST

The night would come down
fierce on my sternum
enough to split and shatter me
I would wake to a thousand pointy shards
spread out across cream sheets
Words afloat like dust particles suspended
in midair
glistening at just-right angles
from the mist of moonlight

What a harsh and breathless way
to wake mid-dream
What a blatant sweet way to tell myself
        I have a bit more left to unhinge today

Soon they would all settle
on the edge of me
teetering
And a clumsy foot race would come forth
to collect them all
But next,
a delicate, precise fitting together
of the meant-to-be

And this is how you bleed heart's ink
This is how you make mosaic out of mess

This is how you take hard broken things
and make poetry

ILLUMINATE

It will not be all sad

Darkness, though it seems
rigid and unbreakable
as it descends on you,
can be shattered by even
the tiniest light

You will find that within you
there is a light, screaming
and that this is the pounding you feel
which is often too much to bear

and that there are a million
ways to cast it out

You will break, but you will see
You will light your own way

Definitions

A mountain of dirt
or a few dark years
do not define
your life

you do

JAR OF YOU

If only life was always easy
like Saturday morning lakeside bench
always magic
like this everywhere soft wind music

But what's always magic is you
I'd like to keep a jar of you
a hand-held capture of all that big joy
Carry it around with me
Let a bit of you out into every moment

In a way I do
like how I see your eyes when I look at bright sky
how I find your earthquake laugh in my Saturday
breakfast
how when it gets dark I just picture
that starlight smile

You'll never know it but
when I look at pitch black tunnels
tall sharp mountains
impossible grey storm
and still feel
strong
capable
bright
it is in part
because of

you

RIGHT BEFORE MY EYES

Where did that face go?
the one I used to admire
and brighten for
and laugh with
When did it melt off like the
weakened flesh of a candle?
How did it happen?
How is it possible that
when I have
looked at it every day
it went from
open sunlight to drawn curtains
without my noticing?

YOU ARE THE POET

Your life is not a tragedy
it is your poem

ORBIT

And just like that
we are back to the start

falling into every space
we fought to leave

We try but never can
keep on in separate ways

After all

love pulls harder
than gravity

MIDDLE SCHOOL

there are tiny
creatures in me

one in my heart
that stomps around

one in my lungs
that drains the air

one in my brain
that erases it all

one in my veins
that punches walls

one in my throat
that cannonballs

whenever it's my turn
to speak

LOOK THROUGH THE LACE

Peace does not always find me in the moment
I suppose it is more of a cloak with holes
than a building

Which is to say that I have peace
draped across my life, softly
but it does not always cover me

And I wish I could say that it is always quiet but
some days I am more scream than anything else

Some days I simply cannot tame
the open-ended shouts in me
this unsettled blue welling up, this wanting

But look

The rain beads up countless hopes across the silky skin
of rose petals
the sky turns itself inside out, twice a day
electric pink

and the wind settles in almost knowingly
brushes the hair from your face, exposes you

There is always, always something
to ground and quiet you
if you just open up and look for it

FROM THE FRINGE

They wonder why I pull away to the edges
It's because I see so much more from here

INEVITABILITY

Despite our stubborn battles
the days do not erase themselves
They linger and sear
call home to the quiet corners
reverberate ceaselessly
And still the hardest memories
are the brightest, are the fondest
The light finds its way, like a snake
around corners, between crevices
across decades to your skin
That streak of sun
through your blinds at daybreak
is not an accidental hello
It is persistence
And that day, a placeholder
that moment, a bookmark
that breath, a reminder
Radiant longing does not settle easily
The inevitable always comes to life
Love will always eventually
break free

Every Damn Time

I would jump right in
to your black sky eyes if I could

and I do

every time
I make myself small to save you

every time
I tell myself this nightmare
is the bitter outer coating of a dream
just needing a touch of sun
or warm lips
to melt through it

every time
I beg you to stay
even though
you always leave

every time
you come back
and I convince myself
you were in good places
all along

every time
you choose sharp needle
but I stay
soft silk in your palms
anyway

CHOOSE THE SKY

Eventually a choice will come and demand itself
answered:

Face the wide open sky
and its layers upon layers of unknown
or keep yourself tucked comfortably
beneath that old familiar ceiling

WHISPER ON CHRISTMAS

You would feel her whisper
from the ugliest part of her throat
that she would tell them all

You would learn the ways
a tiny whisper
can turn to giant knife

how life can suddenly twirl on its toes
inside a holiday afternoon

how certain losses
leave you with extra weight

THE NEXT PAGE

It is when I am still that I am most confused

I settle down
but I am never settled, do you see?

My pulse lifts like the breeze the minute I am still
I pull apart in the quiet
watch the calm pour out of me the way the
sun cuts through branches

I fragment every. single. moment. I am given

And I've never admitted this to anyone
but I am always wishing I was someplace else
always
              waiting

though I am never quite sure for what

I've dreamt of this moment before
wished myself into it
and now that I am here I mostly
disintegrate into my own thoughts, turn myself
outside in

I can't quite explain it.

When it is dark I want white
When it is white
I want to drench myself in black ink
and just bleed into tomorrow

Am I making any sense?

I wonder if I will spend my whole life

in the next room
on the next page

wishing for a world that is
                unfolding right before me
but I never see it
because
I have my eyes squeezed behind a pen
trying to write up better stories
Why can't I ever open my hand
                and
                        just
                                live them?

How Do I Lose You?

The writing has thinned and that
is how I know you are leaving me

But you were never really with me
were you? Never here. Never mine

Except in these pages. Except in a
slender fold of existence, in a mind

But my mind is losing you now too
So where does that leave this(us)?

Tell me,

how do you lose something that's
never been here and always has?

LIFE'S GREATEST TRAGEDY

What a tragic way
to spend a perfectly good life:

Waiting
for its
arrival

EARLY SUMMER PROMISE

Memorize the feeling
of spring unfolding into summer

Like turning a new page
in an old book

and with it an entire layer
is pulled right off the surface of you

Remember how you feel lighter
somehow

and more exposed

Wide open
with places to go

Memorize the explosion of green
and live colors

The feeling
of noticing everything in full bloom

and forgetting how it got there

Remember that you can always start over again
brand new

NEXT COMES GUILT

There will be a new burden suddenly
rested on the slope of your heels
It will come at the depths of your moving on
at that first moment you realize you have begun your
uprising
It will be all sharp and painted with the things
he could have been had you saved him
It will scream at you from the underneath
all the things you should have done so differently
for him
and thrust upon your eyes a relentless film reel
of alternate realities, of could-have-beens

had you only
                tried harder

MUSINGS AT MIDNIGHT

How my breath splits
and turns back to these lungs

How the night sky presses down on me
as I look up at it

How I realize there is nowhere
I can turn and find you
really find you
and yet I feel the weight of you
everywhere

How certain things are so heavy that
only paper can hold them

FOR EVERYTHING (EXTRAORDINARILY) YOU

It can feel so quicksand
tending to this dream-drenched heart
pinned down to tiny paper town

When I start to feel trapped with myself
I think of you in your 10x10 box
how you make continents and oceans out of it
how you never once complain

Did I ever tell you
you have globes instead of eyeballs?
that I think there are a million universes
folded into the small of your chest?

And that laugh
I can hear all of time echoing inside it

I would do anything for that laugh

A billion thank yous would never be enough
for pouring some out just for me
for making me feel infinite on a Sunday afternoon
for giving me the feeling of
existence
swelling up at my feet

for everything you

ON ACCEPTING YOU

I have come to realize
that how you treated me
was never about me

It was always just about you
and your fearful insides

When I look at you now
all I see is a wounded animal
huddled in a corner

And it makes it easier
to hold the fact
that you've hurt me

INNER LANDSCAPE

I have always lived like this, in extremes
When it is bad I dive right in, hollow myself out
let it fill me
But when it is good I pour, stretch it out like sunlight
This landscape will get the most
and hold the best of me
but I will not resent that which is woven in me
and breathes life to poetry

DRIFTWOOD AND BLUSH

One day
underneath the blush of shying sun
or in the tiny sliver of morning
between dark and light
when the honey dimness still hovers
and coats you with dreams
the stone armor dread will evaporate from your skin
and you will realize that
your uncertainty and open sail is not
the scariest thing in this world
but instead
it is all the firm expectations
you anchor yourself to
instead of floating

UNHINGE

Love
is not a loss
It is a
Finding

SHE WILL

She has dreams in her eyes
and magic in her veins

And sunlight streaming through
her fingertips

She will make the tiny things big enough
She will paint the dark things bright white
and yellow

And in every patch of dirt she finds
she will grow wildflowers

WHEN AUTUMN FALLS

Autumn will unfold
like an old trusted map
that upheaves dust
and sparks in you
possibilities
that will cascade out
and float down
make perch across all of your edges
alert your surface
like a crisp cool breeze
emblazon your being
like forest fading deep scarlet red
refresh in you
a sense of ready
of anticipation
of starting over again new
of anything
(even good, even great)
can happen

MELTING

The way your chest grows taut
and then softens
The way I'd like to rest my
bones there

To Be (My Own) Burden

To be everything
is also to be big iron burden
or broken compass
Don't you see two ends of me
are pinched down in opposite locations?
And there is a thinning at my middle
a growing distance
a confusion
a space that can swallow me from inside out if I let it
and a certain gravity building
I have been wasting time as a magnet
instead of an arrow
acquiring when I should have been going
But there have always been
skyscrapers and small towns in me
paper and stone
venom and honey
deep city and shallow coast
all tumbled together with questions
like, when you hold everything
how do you balance? how do you choose?
When you long for everywhere
how do you rest?
and where in the world do you
set yourself down?

REFILL

It won't always be easy
the newness
the emptiness

But empty is also
open

Empty is also
the space for
fresh cool water
to spill

Empty
will always
eventually
become full again

AFTER THE TORNADO

These lungs are strong; this life, fragile
How quickly winds can shift, skies can shatter
worlds can split in two
Let it be known that I warned you:
You will not want the remorse when existence breaks
Calm your racing feet
Do you even know what you are running for?
There is sweet Earth beneath your soles
Let it soothe you
Wake up, you are doing so much only partially alive
Breathe deeper
Have you even noticed?
There is this whole world that can lift
or break
or swallow you
and you are thriving in it
Today smells like evergreen and fresh perspective

SOUL'S WORK

The words come to me at night in the dark
on the bridge just before sleep
Some nights I curl up still
beneath those cotton shields and I hide
Other nights I lay spread out exposed
I listen to the beating of my soul's words
and this is when I hear the most of myself

HERE'S THE THING ABOUT PAIN

Pain cannot be
erased
ignored
covered
hidden
or forgotten

It can only be
transformed

Conundrum

It is a clenched fist
A wet trickle down spine
A gentle tear cascading the round slope of cheek

It is a new paint
drying a color all wrong
It is the swift churn of regret

It is your sharp voice chasing after me
A knife slicing my Achilles as I race up the stairs
And the pillow I collapse into

It is something I will always run from
but always turn back to

It is the black tar I am stuck in
And the shoes I will peel myself out of
and leave behind

It is a burning house
And a home wrapped in rose vines
Both suffocating me

It is the heavy current pushing me away
And the strong wave demanding my return

It is ice cold
And white hot

A broken record
I am sick of hearing
but can't get rid of

A suffocating hug

A scalding sip of my favorite tea

A soft lamb with a lion's bite

It is you

STAND TALL

Stand tall beneath the ever-reaching sky

Do you feel it?
Do you feel it?

You are tiny and you are so immensely
powerful, too

Evermore by the Sea, Evermore You and Me

I say don't hope, execute. We talk about the future
as if we have any say. Maybe we will put up houses
big enough for all of our love and dreams. Maybe I
will simply drift out to sea. Either way, today I am in
Lordship and nowhere else. We sip almond milk from
a mason jar, nibble fresh mango, walk right through a
bend of my past. How does time curve back into itself
like that? Perhaps we put nothing behind us, it all just
folds into the fringes. After all, we are inside this spiral
that does not stop. I'm not even the same as I was a
second ago. But there is a pink house, the end of a
sidewalk, a pulling of the sea within me now. Parts
of me will always be with you on Pauline Street.

YOU: THE SUNSET AIR

You are that moment
just before the sun falls
and the world settles in
like a kept promise

the weightless sense
of being suspended in time
and nestled into the softness
between day and night

You are lighter air
against this skin

THE ONLY WORTHY THING

A heaviness hangs in my space
but I am still free floating
There is a tight fist pulling in the core of me
an unraveling
an openness that in turn closes me

I am wanting for everything
I am going everywhere and nowhere
I am drifting with no ties to the ground yet
still somehow I am this stubborn anchor

Maybe I was made of too much mass
for these dreams trying to stream out of me
Maybe the path that leads to everything
does not exist

I search and search and search
for what will still me yet shake me
hold me yet push me
soothe me yet swirl me

The only worthy thing
I've ever found at the ends of these roads
is me

FREED

To write
is to find a new
layer of free

SORRY COMES FROM WITHIN

It should not be like this
I look for questions, never answers
I plant swords beneath the scars
just to remind myself you put them there
You call and I can't help but
curse the sweetness in your voice
Where was the honey when I was
all gushing wounds and clawing for help?
You can't possibly think
that this is your redemption
It is always too late
when you look at yourself first
and never learn
that sorry comes from your diaphragm
not your lips

How Sad

At the end of a windy country road
in the back corner of a cardboard house
rancid and opaque with smoke
I am trying to erase this war in me

How sad
I think no one could ever understand
what it is like to have dark words
cut across my brain like swords
an explosion of fear pounding against my every surface
for no reason at all
a trembling coldness that rises up like a tide but
never falls

I spent years on mucky fields
sweating out every last pathetic drop of my
shortcomings
tearing apart my own muscle fibers hoping I might
grow back a different girl
while my knees swayed and knocked
like trembling twigs
and they all whispered—*if only there was more to her*

If only there had been more to me, I agree!
inside, outside
everywhere in between

Now he's telling me he loves me in an effortful slur
of his tongue
his eyes nearly closed
face lain against a haggard old couch cushion

There is nearly no life left in him these days
and yet I believe him

Even I know that only an empty someone
would believe a claim like that

Flash back, I am four feet tall
dreaming about new worlds and loves and trophies
I picture a pretty dot on the other side of this map
but I have no idea how to connect myself to it

Instead I lay back and look at the ceiling
struggle to empty my brain
but things keep creeping back in

like
circles, spirals, eyes rolling at me,
a vision of a black hole in my chest,
shadows, a million potential untimely deaths,
all of my oxygen escaping from a pinhole,
a scraped knee from 1997, lost friends

Then, I am a bit older
I learn that these things can be washed away
easily
in the backs of old cars or in deep woods
or in old, dank houses like this one

How sad
I try sex, smoke, alcohol
when what I needed was love

How sad
I had so much swelling up in me
but never thought to give any
                                    to myself

Bitter Coat

As long as I keep blaming you
I will wear a coat in the middle of summer
I will drag buildings behind my shoulders
I will work with cracks in all my bones
and throughout the core of me

and all of my memories
will have dirt smeared across them

It is not a glamorous magic trick
convincing myself
that this is all because of you
when I have always
had control
over me

BLACK AND NARROW PRAYER

I will make myself
warm and silk and cloud

I will float down to your flesh and wrap you
coat you
understand you

I will go back and unravel
this mind's tapestry
of right and wrong

I will re-sew myself to suit your shape
rest better with your sins

I will be light like mid-winter snow
yet warm like sand against your veins

I will be anything

How come no matter
how perfect and soft
and delicate
I drape myself out at your feet
I will never compare
to slick needles
that sew air-tight swaddle?

If I am your light
how come you always choose
dark heavy blanket
instead of
me?

PERSPECTIVES

Maybe
I needed the black
for the contrast

Maybe
the dark also showed me
the light

Returning Home

Where do I even begin?

How do you find the
starting point
of a circle that's already
been drawn?

It is the horizon
an old forgotten tongue
gravity
oxygen
not a beginning or an end
but both
and everything in between
not a start
but a discovery
better yet, an upheaval
energy itself
a promise whispered
into existence and
its echo and
everything it reaches

It is returning home
It has always been here

What I mean is
when you first touched me
somehow I had felt your
hands before

THE WATER

You fall like buildings
rise like fire

At the top of every exhale
your words (quick, heavy)
escape like stampedes

Always the worst first
Always swift to cut me

Always I must find the gentle in me

SING HER HOME

There was a splendor of skies wedged into her irises
or maybe they were hopes
or the first moments of a rainstorm
Regardless, it all feels the same across your skin
a release, a whisper

a fresh start

It had come to a point where she had to turn her eyes
upside down just to look at her own life
and how in all the pretty corners there was unfair
poison hovering

how their hands could erase the past
even the happy in it
how their shadows covered the light for miles on end

She would go far to escape it all
build a new home
a life
a strength

a strength that had always been there
but had been quieted with time
pressed down by their palms

a strength she would find
unexpectedly
inside a lazy afternoon
when the sun would graze her face just so

and she would realize that she was the only home
she ever needed

THINK TWICE

Of all the things to do with pain
                    why cast it at someone else?

Simultaneous

I have had you
infinitely inside tiny scattered moments

and

I have had you
never at all

It has been both
more than enough

and

overwhelmingly inadequate
all at once

SKIN AND BONES

Perhaps there was not enough of me to begin with
Between the skin and the bones
I was mostly whispers and insecure hope

We would watch our friends put out flames
with bare fingers
Drink cheap vodka from the bottle
Roll down the windows
and smile as our hands cut the air
We laughed at all the things that should have mattered

In between these moments I would fall flat
There was nothing like the swelling
when we were together
Every time I left you it was like introducing me
to myself again
I fought to find who was there but I was
nowhere to be seen

I foolishly made up new definitions of myself
The inhale at the start of your laugh
The girl inside your best dream
Or maybe the twitch that kept you up, I did not care

Every acceptable version of myself I could possibly
write had you in it

You were working to erase me from your story while I
was trying to insert you between every line
As if you should have been the very flesh
between my skin and bones

As if I was not the right person to fill in my own blanks
but you were

We would crawl back to each other when it all
got to be too tiring
Try to flood the cracks, though it was never lasting
We moved mountains
to make this exactly how we thought it should be

Except our plans were never the same from the start

I wanted you to fill me and I ended up empty
You wanted to crack me open so this wouldn't be
your fault
Instead you broke

Quiet Is Not What Empty Looks Like

With so many beautiful words
that make even the more beautiful sentences
and paragraphs
and poems
I find it hard to speak anything unless it is perfect
and so I often sit quiet
and they assess me as stupid
or scared
or empty
or all of the above

Well, maybe I am stupid
for letting these thoughts escape
unsaid
and thus, not to be remembered

And maybe I am scared
of being imperfect
(or worse)

But empty?
Oh, please

I am
overflowing

POST-TRAGEDY

How bittersweet to live on with the reality
that our hearts are strong enough
to beat us through the thick of hardship
yet delicate enough
to be stopped at any time

REGENERATION

But maybe that's just
how it will go:

break
and
re-grow

break
and
re-grow

I See Yellow

The steering wheel and a throbbing in my ear
I am flat in a bleeding world today
so I drive
upward along the sharpest edge, chase the sky
I fumble with definitions
I realize
this swelling beneath my skin
is one part confusion, one part anticipation,
one part I cannot quite name,
but it is something and it is wild today
I can't help feeling that I know the curves
of these roads
I have lived in these houses
I have drowned in this exact moment before
I inhale everything at once, but that amounts to
nothing
I close my eyes and, somehow, I see yellow
I ask the sun
how it rises every morning with such confidence
knowing it can never reach everything at once
And what happens if,
despite my fraying grasp,
I want more than half a world at a time?

CHOSEN ONE

You can't help it

You pour white light
into the cracks of my voice

as it breaks against the silence
I thrust on this tongue

I coax sweet words to the forefront
wrestle them back hard

Breathe in the bitter, deep

I can't help but crumble
and wonder
at all of the unfairness in this

Restraint is a difficult beast
it is only for the chosen few

The ones who always break
and hold it together

just the same

A PROMISE TO MYSELF

If the walls of my life
must be white
then I will hang miracles upon them

HEALING SOLO

The after you is all open and cold with relief
It is a harsh, unfamiliar thing
but I must bear it

There is no rulebook for leaving, so I will
make things up while I go

I run until my legs scream
and my heart flings itself from my chest
I study until there is no room in my brain
for you
And when these do not work
I peel frosty words off my tongue
and throw them at paper
call it poetry

This does not feel like art
it feels ugly
It feels like I left someone to die
and then turned it into a sexy story
like I am on a fast plane up to the clouds
and you are a speck in my window
—*Bye!*

This poetry
it warms me but as soon as my hands rest
the cold, guilty truth spreads back through me
that you are suffering and I am
healing

CHERRY BLOSSOM

Be kind
to life

even when
it is not kind
to you

In This Limestone Skin

It is like there is a force field around you
He said
and it is hard for anyone to get in

I know, I feel it too

What do you think it is like on the inside?

I used to pound at it with open palms
Throw a shoulder up against it
uncalculated, but with assault

This took energy
and sanity
and many of the good things

and was wildly ineffective

Now, I am using tools
to chisel away at one spot
slowly, but meticulously
and surely

I know it won't be long now
until I am officially broken free

This force field is no match
for a force like me

DESPERATE MESSAGE

I am an unsealed envelop
Put the filthy words in me
your dusty secrets
Whisper them in heart's ink
I promise they are safe with me

I want more than sharp ends of stories
dirty results of your history I have
been soiled with

I want the bloody reasons

THE PRICE OF LONGING

I am clenched breath
and cracked chest
where these truths sit heavy
There is nothing like the weight
of what you cannot have

WILDFIRE

I am sprawled out thin in a moonlit room
Paper-flat, my spine
but belly bloated with too many hot words that will not
find the surface
I was thirst and rust and cold breath
not long ago,
when I touched the ocean floor
and came up screaming for darker air—*Save. Me.*
But I wanted it warm.
I wanted it forty days ago
when the sun spread longer and I hid
I wanted it all the way out to the horizon,
too far to reach
Because here is where I do best, always:
I slither for the edges
I unstitch seams
I pull the gentle light from these walls
and bring it to flames
I search for windows. Everywhere.   Escape doors.
And I am always one foot through them
I am never fully here.
Even in this moonlit room, even in this still, slow glow
when I am safe space, soft pen, dry paper
and steady light
I am also a raging wildfire just outside the house
     spreading   fast   and   violent.

UPRISING

My eyes are
          flash
                    floods

when I think of you

not because I am sad
but because

it was so sad
     and ugly
          and breaking

down there with you

but somehow
I crawled out

                    more me

SNOWFALL

And at once
winter will remind us
that strength can be found
in falling
True beauty has no hue
There is wonder
in wiping slates clean

Rewrite History

I close my eyes against the sting of your words
I paint myself back to a time when you were softer and
there was more life in your hands

All of the open wounds that existed then have since
healed over
Now there is a more hardened you, but not stronger

I watched you throw yourself into an ocean
proclaim you did not know how to swim
aspirate until you exhaled poison

But the drowning is just a trick
you play on yourself to keep from feeling

You lost essential pieces in the downfall
I lost a feeling I can only describe as home

My eyes peel open when your words relent
It is a filthy warmth that hangs here in their absence

I think how nothing will ever shrink this space in me

Hesitantly, I nod, smile softly
pluck the words "I know" from the base of my tongue
kiss comfort in your direction

Inside I scream

I do not want sorry.
I want you to wave your hands and make it so this
never happened

I want you to go back and keep yourself from falling
apart at the thought of your life collapsing
when you should have been thinking of me

I want you to rewrite history
I want there to be nothing to be sorry for

I want you to have saved yourself for me

ROSE BERRY

The way she glows
gives new meaning to bright

She is cut from the fabric of starlight
topped with pure sun flare curls

But brightest of all is that spirit
wild warm like forest fire

Even the glacier hearts melt themselves to oceans
just for her

THE DIFFERENCE BETWEEN US

You wrote me
a note once
in serpent's tongue
across my back

It told me I have
never in my life
been loved
to the depths
that I deserve

I have written
you so many notes
since then
folded them into
oblivion
watched them burn

You are still
the thing for which
my heart will rue
and quiet
and soften

The difference
between
us is where we
put our words

INTROVERT

I am strongest
    at the soft, quiet parts

THE ONLY PLACE WHERE WE FIT

Meet me in the shades of grey
in the moments just before nightfall
where lines blur
and the world loses depth
Meet me where sky fades to stone
I'll be waiting there on the bridge
between right and wrong

I Become an Echo

How can I put this?

There is an
unraveling
a sense of
spiraling
into layered sky

Have you felt the
build
as winter
collapses
into spring?

the release
of summer
igniting
autumn's hymn?

and the way it all
stretches
against the curves
of living?

Have you felt the
brush of time
erase and add
between
breaths and blinks?

and the way that
blooms something
in us?

Then you have felt
the moment
just after your eyes
leave mine,

the infinities
fluttering
beneath my ribcage,

the stampede that
simultaneously
bulges and vanishes,

the thrill of
being pulled open
and left
echoing anew

MY LIFE

There is serenity in the fact
that I hold the pieces to this puzzle

AFTERMATH AND GIN

How do I handle this
sweetness
muddled with guilt?

I've never navigated
anything like
the aftermath of you

I drown in the question of
do you miss me
or was I nothing at all?

AVALANCHE

This winter has been the longest yet, all hollow and
tepid. Not even ice, not even frozen. More melting
than anything else

In other words, there is less of me now

I jumped off these pages, out of this book. What is the
opposite of acceptance? What could this be called?

I screamed good-bye to history, as if it ever leaves.
Took a torch to every hope. And, perhaps worst of all,
watched a million futures evaporate into the color-
drained sky

I did not realize all of the glaciers I had been carrying
on this chest. All of the expectations, heavy against my
skin. How they anchored me, how they defined me

How they would feel in ruins at my feet

There is less of me now. Let it echo. Let it ring. Set off
an avalanche. I am the stampeding snow. I am stark
white canvas, hollow as this winter. I am the heavy
pen, upright, bleeding into every space

I am all new stories now

BLACK SWEATER

Your biggest flaw
is that you look at the less-than-good in them
as making them *all* bad

As if you do not have a few dark threads
woven in you, too

EMPTY

When I look at you
I see only a massive emptiness

I see that sometimes
life can give you everything but
still drain you dry

that sometimes
you try so hard to rid the bad
you lose the good too

that the empty can be so heavy
it cracks your bones and
shears your skin

I see so many heart-clenching truths
but still have not found
one answer:

Is empty really better than hurting?

INSTRUCTIONS FOR HEALING

Find a thing of meaning
and importance
to pour yourself into

and in return
life will pour
into you

NEVER YOURS

Trace the edges of me
like small town border
golden grain coast
I am the everything in between
the lush fields you drove past in your youth
the firm soil foundation beneath your soles
I will make you feel home and natural
Lift you up by my slopes
and roll me down
I will be open plain for you
I will be flourishing forest you get lost in
I am the real life inside plastic dream globe
The organic taste you search for
I am rich full Earth
and you can write maps of me
climb me like harsh stone mountain
explore me in your everyday
But I will never be completely
yours

Drenched

I don't look at it much
but somewhere down deep in me
there is a thick wet hurt
with your name drenched in it

A Sort of Thank You

I wish you could see
how all the broken bits of me
have made the loveliest of art pieces

If you are the sword
that sliced me up into pieces,
trim and tiny,
then I am the gentle hand
that sewed together a quilted masterpiece

If you are the fist
that made a mess of me
then I am the genius
who made a mosaic out of it

Light reflects brilliantly off me now
I just had to say

If you are the chemical
that broke my words into nothing but particles
or letters
then I am the patient artist who collected them all

and made poetry

REBIRTH

You will continue
to shed and lose and learn
to hurt at the unfinished parts
and to break at the ones
that need releasing

Sharp, Sweet Knowing

hope shivers
a flickering flame
in the dark

night
a hand that creeps
that takes more than
it leaves

yesterday
a bulky cloak
spread thick across
the window

but there is gold
against
the shadows

honey
somewhere
in the hollow

strength inside
the jelly center
of the
certainty of
hurt

I am still now
unraveling

spun
strong and effortless
shimmering
with the wind

a calm breath
that goes where it
is blown
without fear

on the balmy
waves
of memory

of knowing
there is nothing
that time will not
eventually
take from me

Silence Becomes an Ocean

If only you knew of the waterfalls in me
The oceans
The depths I have gone to
to make space for a love that just can't fit
and keep it hidden

The burden of quiet on these lips

To Live, Fully

Learn the art of balancing
the holding on
and the letting go

The Only Reason

Wheels glide outside my window intermittently, just like outside number sixty-three next to the bridge, where you were more alive, or at least appeared to be

I'd like to pinpoint when it all went wrong, see it up close, stare it in the eye, confront it in a quiet alley

What was it made of, the thing that caused your collapse?

What was your reason?

I'm starting to forget there was ever a before. But that is the bitter artwork of time. Nothing goes untouched. Lines blur. Memories bleed into one another. Moments turn to moments turn to fog

All I am left with now is a vision of you that tastes like wreckage

It is a melting candle. A drawn face. A coffee stain on fresh linen. Wet flesh between molars. A pit in the throat. The edge of a cliff. A giant question mark. A greasy water color. The shedding of skin. Fatigue. It is you

It is your face. Echoing in each corner. Reflecting against every wall. And these tired hands, the hands of a puzzle-master. They have re-arranged every segment, switched out every piece. Still it is your face. Still it is you

These hands are tired. This realization, exhausting. It
has pulled the life with it on its way out of me

That moment I mentioned before, the one I have spent
a thousand Thursdays trying to pinpoint. It is not a
moment after all. It was never a moment. It was never
a happening, or an event, or a monster. It was you

You are your only reason

ARE YOU ALIVE?

If you think the growing
comes to a point and stops
you are wrong

If you are alive
you should be growing

If you are not growing then
are you truly living?

SIMPLE DREAMS

In my dreams
you are always whole
dressed in old soft white t-shirt
full heart bulging through
drenched in the happiest blood
and peace
with sincere apologies
dripping from your lips
I am sorry
I am sorry
I am sorry
In my dreams
I am smiling through child's face
holding out a heavy heart drum
that beats solid love for you
and no resentment
There is so much sweet
and none of the bitter
In my dreams
I forgive you
over and over and over again
and always

LIGHT IN FLESH AND BLOOD

Don't let them tell you
you are sad
because you write hard sharp words
that cut true

You are not dark
you are brilliant
You are not emotion
you are light in flesh and blood
You are not transient
you are long lasting strength

You are not sad
you are the thing that comes after
the thing that has no name
but looks a lot like
peace

DEEP WELLS

The pain will always be there
in deep wells
waiting to be drawn out
and poured
into something else

Know you can always go there
to take
and then
make better

BLOOM, DESPITE

Shadows falling
not fading, falling suddenly

And not a graceful separation
a dropped plate
a heavy heart, shattered
a severed branch in a thunderstorm

And their shadows only leave when
their light goes away
or they lose their substance

Either way, it's devastating
Either way, it's a loss

Before I know it they are sheet metal
smooth, but stark cold
unmoving
Tombstones in fresh cut grass
cemented
trapped in the sticky fog of their own aching

But I am a soft hand on trampled glass
the flower in the graveyard
Out of place
but nevertheless placed there
Sunset yellow against gloom
and starving for out
starving for up and away

I can't waste time waiting for the why
or the gust of wind to take me away

I dig in my heels
plant my feet like roots

let the tears water me
let the tears lift me up

up to the edge of the sky
up to the warm sunlight

and I bloom

even in the charcoal fog
I bloom

TRANSFORMATION

In realizing
I could never change you
I changed myself

REMEDY

For a moment
I let these bones soften
It has been a season of labor
of kneading at all of the
frail, swollen places
and re-working soil to strength
I let that all settle now
with the crest of my spine
Rest back, although
I know this calm is fleeting
Beg the sun to warm me
to help me for once
melt this mind into present
and I drink in the sky as if
there would ever be a remedy
for restlessness

COMPLETE

Life is a thread
slim and fragile
Perpetual, really

Though, since it trails off into the horizon
and blurs out
we lose track of it

become obsessed with tracing
its length

And we squint
and strain
until our eyes become fixed
and pinched at the corners
and mostly closed
and glued to the line

until all surroundings are lost from view

And so we just don't realize:
The beads are what matter
The beads
the moments
the atoms of life

It's the whole point of the thread, anyway

Look around
find the best ones
pick them out like flowers in a field

Make them yours

String them together
one by one
until you look along and realize:

you've made something
so beautiful you can be
complete

MAPS

We are all just searching for something
that will ignite us like adventure
and calm us like home

How Can I Keep You Smiling?

Most days I forget the
way things (you) used to be
and that is what we call
                              surviving

But what about us walking
side by side summer evening
how you'd make me laugh
like a volcano
all of that sweetness
all of those years

How do I erase one thing
              and keep the other

Tell me
how can I put the black
next to white
stop them from seeping
avoid the grey

choose what I wish to see to
keep you laughing

                         smiling

sweet

              in all my yesterdays

Please
   tell me it can work like that

MINE

There is something to be said about holding your love
silently. It is an itching power, a key in a lock, unturned

I could paint the sky with this burning red if I wanted,
set the world aflame above me, send out a war cry; or I
could simply let this bleed itself through me. In the end
it is all mine for the deciding and the tending

I am the keeper and the key and the lock and the home
I am the only one who must bare this

Early on I swallowed it whole, banished it to the
marrow, told it to make itself comfortable. And it has
crept into the matter, it will blossom in these bones

You would not know it, but there is a fire in me. Heaps
of scarlet petals rushing up beneath my skin

Still you could not pry this out of me if you tried.

I will tell you one thing, these limbs are stronger for
treating love as a souvenir, not a give-away, when it is
wrong

and you cannot break the heart that decides it is a
safe-house.

WHAT CATCHES THE LIGHT

You see
there is a corner of existence
where light ricochets
and reality tumbles into space
I wonder what of all this matters
If I was to die tomorrow
I would go with
almosts braided into my hair
an unfinished
book on my chest
the echo of unfair along these lips
There is so much that
needs fixing
Wouldn't it be lovely
to kick that all over the edge and
see what catches the light?
I have a feeling that
not much would end up in my hands
I am realizing I need to be lighter
and louder yet
find a stone to hold these hopes
and carve them
Who am I if I am not someone
I would die for?

EVERGREEN

Meet me at the edge of existence
I'll be waiting there
beneath the evergreens
with soft shoulders
and hard love on these hands
Sit with me as I cry out at the horizon
for all of the answers
for how in the world there can be
born a love so wide
and be no room for it

No Small Thing

And today beneath the smile
of afternoon sun
I will say it once and for all:
    you have been good

I am not sure why this has been
the hardest whisper when it has
    always been so loud and clear

I would say sorry for this stubborn
soul if you had not
    been the one to gift it to me

Yes, you have given me this grit

these soft hands, these eyes like sky
this headstrong persistence, this
    fickle, escalating heart

And you know this all amounts to
    everything

Yes, today I will say it once and for all:
you have given me everything
    and that is nothing small

HUMAN

She moved into the light
and her scars glittered

THIS INCREDIBLE GIFT

You may not say it but I can
still feel your soul thanking me
in every sweet moment when
I feel the sun a little warmer
or notice how it fragments
vibrantly off flower petals,
a kaleidoscope of gratitude

or how I've never seen the hue
of your eyes before, except in
the sky, and how that silky ocean
water is actually your skin,
the shaking wind, your laugh

or when I feel my chest stiffen
and I can somehow take more breath in
close my eyes, see the possibilities
remember all the details
that have always been there but
I've never noticed before

and, let me say this loudly
if this gift is the only
one you ever give me it will still
be more than enough,
to have shown me that living,
truly living,
is to breathe deep, to notice
to drift in the quiet moments, and
to love in a way that never
thinks of yourself

LUCKY

Exhale into the morning sun
Look up and let it remind you
you are lucky

MOSAIC

When all is said and done I find myself a quiet corner
fold into it sweetly

I hang frames around the things that should have been
toss them all from the highest window

If life has not been what you expected
then that is perfect, you are living

If there have been dark days
I think you ought to thank the skies for the contrast

My life has been blood red
buried black, amaranthine blue

avalanche white
sunset yellow, electric pink

and a grey I can only describe
as suffocating

Here is what I have learned:
If you want it all to make more sense then take a big
step back

The difference between mistake and masterpiece
is sharper eyes
The difference between mess and mosaic
is a careful hand

The difference between surviving and living
is knowing how it all goes together

ATLANTA

This world will keep spinning beneath my feet
so I will go forward, weightlessly, on deliberate toes
dance against the unpredictable wind
toss my head back under the sun
laugh at this fear as it rises up in me,
at this grief for all that was yesterday
but will never be again
hold my arms out for everything unfolding
smile and let it come to me
exhale and let it be

A NEW PLACE

One day you will run up the stairs
like you did when you were a kid
the pads of your naked toes smacking each stair
flesh to wood
like smooth black ice beneath feet
as quick and impatient
as the excited beat of galloping horse hooves
Except now it will not be someone's voice
or a ghost
or the push of darkness
chasing you
You will not be running from
but towards
You will be in a place where the running happens
only to meet something waiting for you
You will be in a place where things will be waiting for
you at the top of the stairs
good things
You will feel like you have been running forever
when you get there
And that last step will be like
hugging a long lost friend
returning to a childhood home
exhaling a long trapped breath

finding the one you've been searching for

realizing that the one you've been searching for
is you

ACKNOWLEDGMENTS

Thank you to my sisters, Lauren Kelly and Emily Forcier, for everything, and to Erin Gribben and Katie Mirabella for your invaluable help.

Made in the USA
Columbia, SC
16 August 2020